SPY GUIDE

SPY SURVEILLANCE

ELSIE OLSON

Abdo & Daughters
MIDDLE GRADE NONFICTION

An imprint of Abdo Publishing
abdobooks.com

ABDOBOOKS.COM

Published by Abdo Publishing, a division of ABDO, PO Box 398166, Minneapolis, Minnesota 55439.

Abdo & Daughters™ is a trademark and logo of Abdo Publishing.

Printed in the United States of America, North Mankato, Minnesota
052024
092024

THIS BOOK CONTAINS RECYCLED MATERIALS

Design: Kelly Doudna, Mighty Media, Inc.
Production: Mighty Media, Inc.
Editor: Katherine Chu
Cover Photographs: AP Images, Flickr, Shutterstock Images, Wikimedia Commons

Interior Photographs: Adobe Stock, p. 13; Alamy Photo, pp. 23, 37; AP Images, p. 16 (top); Flickr, pp. 16 (bottom), 35, 36, 39, 46, 54, 61 (top left); Library of Congress, pp. 24–25, 27, 60 (top right); National Security Agency, p. 8; Shutterstock Images, pp. 1, 4–5, 6–7, 10–11, 15, 17, 40, 41, 45, 53, 56, 57, 58, 59; Wikimedia Commons, pp. 9, 12, 18–19, 20, 21, 26, 28, 29, 30–31, 32, 33, 34, 42–43, 44, 48–49, 50–51, 52, 55, 60 (top left, top middle, bottom left, bottom right), 61 (top middle, top right, bottom left, bottom right)

Design Elements: Adobe Stock

Library of Congress Control Number: 2023949218

Publisher's Cataloging-in-Publication Data
Names: Olson, Elsie, author.
Title: Spy surveillance / by Elsie Olson
Description: Minneapolis, Minnesota : Abdo Publishing, 2025 | Series: Spy guide | Includes online resources and index.
Identifiers: ISBN 9781098293185 (lib. bdg.) | ISBN 9798384912453 (ebook)
Subjects: LCSH: Electronic surveillance--United States--Juvenile literature. | Unauthorized interception of communications--Juvenile literature. | Internet in espionage--Juvenile literature. | Espionage--Juvenile literature. | Spies--Juvenile literature.
Classification: DDC 327.12--dc23

CONTENTS

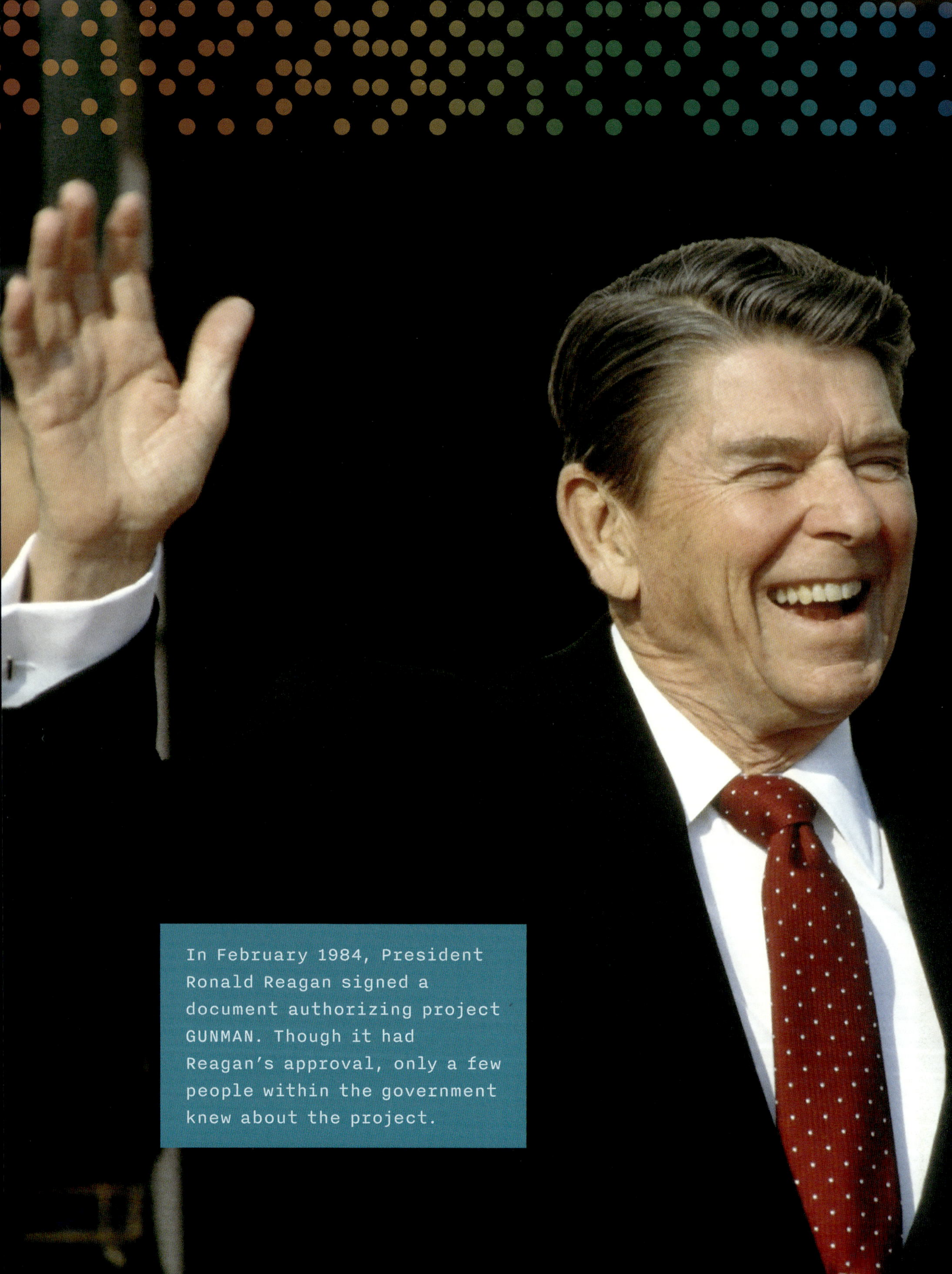

In February 1984, President Ronald Reagan signed a document authorizing project GUNMAN. Though it had Reagan's approval, only a few people within the government knew about the project.

CHAPTER 1

CHASING LEAKS

IT'S 1984, AND ELECTRICAL ENGINEER CHARLES GANDY JUST landed in Moscow, the capital of the Union of Soviet Socialist Republics (USSR), or Soviet Union. It's the height of the Cold War, and the Soviets have gained access to secret information from the US embassy in Moscow. US president Ronald Reagan wants this problem solved. Gandy works for the US National Security Agency (NSA). And he's in Moscow to discover how secrets are being stolen from the embassy.

The Cold War has been a war of information between the US and its allies and the USSR and its allies. But now the USSR seems to have an advantage. US intelligence officials aren't sure how their information is getting out. Many suspect the Soviets planted a bug at the US embassy. Bugs are covert listening devices that can detect and record conversations. US officials know the Soviets are good at planting highly effective bugs. However, regular scans for transmitting devices have come up empty.

BACK IN MOSCOW

This wasn't Gandy's first time at the US embassy in Moscow. During his last bug-hunting trip six years ago, Gandy's team discovered a secret room hidden inside a chimney. It held a mysterious antenna that could be raised or lowered using pulleys. But what was it for? Who was it listening to?

After Gandy's first search of the US embassy in Moscow (*pictured*), the Central Intelligence Agency (CIA) and the State Department stopped him from investigating further because they didn't find evidence of any bugs during their routine scans.

Gandy suspected the antenna was picking up radio signals from devices transmitting inside the embassy. His scans of the building didn't find any suspicious devices or bugs, but he recorded a series of unusual clicks and pops. Gandy didn't know what they meant, so he returned to the US with more questions than answers.

Despite the lack of evidence from his previous trip, Gandy knew US embassy officials were under secret surveillance. He just didn't know how. For the last six years, US security and intelligence agencies had prevented Gandy from continuing his search. They did not believe there were any bugs in the embassy. But after France found a similar bug in their Moscow embassy, Reagan approved a thorough inspection of the US embassy and its equipment.

PROJECT GUNMAN

Gandy started by ordering all 11 tons (10 mt) of electronic equipment at the embassy to be shipped back to the US. There, thousands of pieces were scanned using X-ray technology, taken apart, and carefully inspected, with nothing suspicious found. Then, an X-ray technician made a startling discovery. He noticed a small wire coil inside one of the

Gandy was authorized to continue his search after France found a bug inside its embassy's teleprinters. France told the US, who then launched the GUNMAN project.

typewriters' power switches. Further inspection revealed a shocking truth. For the last eight years, 16 of the embassy's typewriters had sent every single word typed to Soviet intelligence agencies.

Every typewriter contained a solid metal bar that provided structural support. However, the bugged typewriters had an identical-looking hollow metal bar containing a circuit board and

The Soviets' bugs were hidden inside 16 IBM Selectric II (*pictured*) and III typewriters. The bug could only be found through an X-ray scan.

sensors instead. This equipment recorded every keystroke, also known as keylogging. Metal parts of the typewriter, such as springs and screws, were repurposed as antennae and circuit components. The recorded keystroke information was encrypted and sent to a hidden Soviet antenna via radio waves.

The radio transmissions used the same frequency as Soviet television stations, hiding the transmissions from US scanners. But Soviet intelligence agencies could extract and decode the transmissions. The mystery was solved. Rather than being upset, Gandy was impressed by his Soviet counterparts, saying he felt a "kinship" with them.

The most challenging part of secret surveillance is stealing information without the enemy realizing it's missing. This can be done by taking photos of secret documents.

CHAPTER 2

CLANDESTINE COLLECTION

THE BUGGED TYPEWRITERS GANDY'S TEAM DISCOVERED WERE a prime example of secret surveillance. This is the act of stealing secret information from a rival, such as a foreign government or intelligence agency. The Soviets' typewriter bug was also one of the first examples of keylogging technology used for espionage. This meant that the Soviets improved their secret surveillance technology. If the US wanted to keep up with its rival, it would have to do the same.

COVERT OBSERVATION

Secret surveillance is also the art of clandestinely observing an adversary's activities to gain intelligence, or secret information. Intelligence can be gathered by covertly taking photos or video footage of a rival's activities. Intelligence agencies may secretly eavesdrop on, or even record, conversations and phone calls. And spies

US INTELLIGENCE SOURCES

The US government relies on five main methods to gather intelligence. These are sometimes called intelligence collection disciplines. Different government agencies lead each discipline.

OPEN SOURCE

ALL AGENCIES

Gathers information from widely available sources, such as television, radio, newspapers, online articles, research papers, and public records

HUMAN INTELLIGENCE

AGENCIES: FEDERAL BUREAU OF INVESTIGATION (FBI), DOMESTIC INTELLIGENCE; CENTRAL INTELLIGENCE AGENCY (CIA), FOREIGN INTELLIGENCE

Gathers information from human sources

MEASUREMENTS AND SIGNATURES INTELLIGENCE

AGENCY: DEFENSE INTELLIGENCE AGENCY

Gathers information from weapons and industrial activities

SIGNALS INTELLIGENCE

AGENCY: NATIONAL SECURITY AGENCY (NSA)

Gathers information from electronic transmissions, such as phone calls, satellite communications, and online correspondence

IMAGERY INTELLIGENCE

AGENCY: NATIONAL GEOSPATIAL-INTELLIGENCE AGENCY

Gathers information from photos and satellite images

have been known to steal correspondence such as emails, letters, or text messages from other governments or intelligence agencies.

SPIES 101

Surveillance is at the heart of espionage. Modern espionage often uses advanced technology, such as drones, spy planes, and satellites. But spies are still an important part of human intelligence (HUMINT). Some HUMINT is gathered openly through interviews. Other information is collected covertly through spies.

Spies can influence people and situations around them to gain valuable intelligence in a way that surveillance technology cannot. They can ask questions, lead conversations, and develop personal relationships with high-value contacts, known as targets. A good spy may even earn the target's trust, sometimes turning them, or convincing them to spy against their own government.

No matter how effective a spy is, the best intelligence is backed by hard evidence, such as documents, photographs, or audio recordings. This is where surveillance comes in.

Successful spies use their intelligence and skills to watch their targets without getting caught.

SPIES EVERYWHERE

Almost anyone can become a spy. The most important quality for a spy to have is access to secret information. But that doesn't mean a spy needs to be high up in a military, government, or intelligence organization. Spies can be relatives of diplomats, cafeteria workers, or nannies. Anyone in a position to covertly gather intelligence can be a spy.

SIGNALS INTELLIGENCE AND CYBER SPIES

Much of modern surveillance relies on signals intelligence (SIGINT). This involves intercepting electronic signals that may come from communications equipment, weapons systems, or radar. In the US, the NSA is responsible for gathering SIGINT.

Signals are either digital or analog. Analog signals include sound, radio, and television waves. Computers, watches, mobile phones, and tablets use digital signals. Using signals, cyber spies can gain access to devices from thousands of miles away to observe their activity. The NSA can use these signals to listen to cell phone calls, turn off a foreign military's defense equipment, and sometimes even cause a weapon to self-destruct.

More sensitive electronic signals are encrypted, so once a signal is intercepted, it must be decoded. The NSA employs more than one thousand talented codebreakers, scientists, engineers, and mathematicians who work to decrypt messages alongside supercomputers.

The NSA also pays attention to who is signaling whom and the amount of signals going back and forth. This is called traffic analysis.

NSA Hawaii (*pictured*) is a cryptologic center that gathers SIGINT from foreign communication networks and systems. It also protects US communications.

Even if the NSA isn't able to intercept and decode the signals, an increase in volume and frequency can provide clues about a government's or terrorist organization's intentions. With supercomputers, drones, and spy satellites, modern surveillance techniques can feel like science fiction. But the art of surveillance goes back as far as spying itself. And spying wasn't always so high-tech.

THE CHAIN OF INTELLIGENCE

Once a piece of intelligence is collected and decoded, it goes to analysts. They review the intelligence, compare it with other information, and determine if it is reliable. The analysts send a report with the intelligence to decision-makers. These may be lawmakers, military leaders, or even the president! The decision-makers decide how, or if, they will respond to the intelligence.

TOOLS OF THE TRADE: EYES AND EARS EDITION

OFFICE OF TECHNICAL SERVICE

The Office of Technical Service (OTS) is a CIA department dedicated to creating modern spy gadgets. Many of these gadgets conceal high-tech espionage devices in everyday objects. A camera might be hidden in a pen. A coat button might contain a secret recording device. And a mobile phone might include lie detection software. To protect its spies, most of the OTS creations are highly classified. Very few people know exactly what the OTS is working on.

HEEL TRANSMITTER

During the Cold War, KGB agents secretly put a microphone and transmitter in a US diplomat's shoe while it was being repaired.

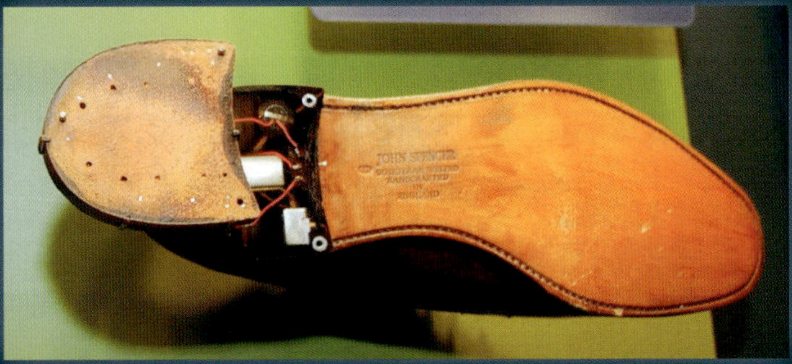

The KGB used this device in the 1960s. The transmitter was activated when a white pin was pulled from the heel of the shoe.

INSECTOTHOPTER

The CIA put microphones in tiny insect-shaped drones in the 1970s. As technology improved, these drones became even more convincing!

The Insectothopter was the first micro unmanned aerial vehicle created by the CIA. Unfortunately, it was too difficult to control, so it was not used in any actual spy missions.

TREE STUMP LISTENING DEVICE

The CIA put equipment inside a fake tree stump to intercept communication and radio signals. In the 1970s, the CIA hid the stump in a wooded area near a Soviet air base in Moscow.

The stump listening device was solar powered and looked like a real tree stump. The CIA used a satellite to retrieve the information collected by the device.

BUG DETECTOR

During the Cold War, the Soviets used a scanner to search for bugs hidden in walls and objects. The detector was revolutionary because it could sense surveillance devices even when they were switched off.

WIRE

These tiny microphones and transmitters can be hidden inside clothing. They allow agents to secretly record conversations.

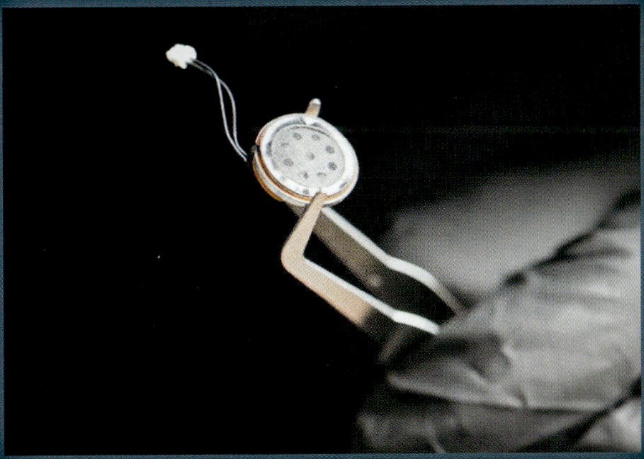

Wearing a wire is risky for spies. There can be severe consequences if they are caught with the device.

King Louis XIV was also known as the Sun King. His reign was known as *Le Grand Siècle*, or "the Great Century."

CHAPTER 3

EARLY SURVEILLANCE

IN 1643, LOUIS XIV BECAME KING OF FRANCE. AT THE TIME, France was the largest and wealthiest nation on Earth. Its powerful military was respected and feared across Europe.

Thanks to his country's success, Louis XIV had many enemies, both inside and outside of France. He was committed to maintaining France's powerful status, and assuring his own rule remained secure. But to do so, he had to know what his enemies were saying.

During his reign, Louis XIV set up a complex intelligence gathering system. He wanted to keep an eye on his enemies and friends, so he scattered spies in major cities across Europe. His spies read people's private letters, giving Louis XIV access to their private communications.

In the 1600s, letters were used for all long-distance correspondence. Spies intercepted and read letters written by officials, nobility, or anyone suspicious, sending the intelligence back to Louis XIV. Some of these people soon realized

King Louis XV (*pictured*) used King Louis XIV's system of reading and analyzing letters. The system became officially known as the *cabinet noir*, or "black chamber."

he was reading their correspondence and began coding their letters, so Louis XIV employed codebreakers to decrypt them. This system alerted Louis XIV of potential threats and the military operations of his enemies. By the 1670s, Louis XIV's army was the best in the world, largely thanks to his intelligence gathering operation.

LOW-TECH SURVEILLANCE

While King Louis XIV was famous for his dedication to intelligence gathering and espionage, he didn't invent the spying techniques he used. In the late 1500s, Queen Elizabeth I used spies to intercept her cousin Mary Stuart's letters. And espionage and surveillance have been around as long as civilization itself.

But before the 1800s, surveillance was low-tech. Intercepting letters was a popular surveillance method, but it wasn't the only means of surveillance used by early spies.

Many of King Louis XIV's spies were women, such as Louise de Kéroualle. She helped Louis XIV by gathering intelligence on King Charles II of England.

SPIES EVERYWHERE

HUMINT was an ideal way to gather intelligence before electronic communications equipment was invented. Early spies eavesdropped on conversations, listening through doors and windows. They wore disguises and listened to conversations in pubs or restaurants. Some spies even owned businesses where people frequently gathered, such as shops or hotels. These spies were in a perfect position to listen to conversations around them without raising suspicion.

Some of the best early spies were those underestimated by society, including women and racial minorities. During the American

ENSLAVED SPIES

During the American Revolution, many key pieces of intelligence came from Black spies enslaved by Loyalists, supporters of the British cause. One such spy was a man named Quaco. He was enslaved by British Loyalist James Honeyman, who lived in Rhode Island. Honeyman often rented Quaco out to work for British officers. In 1777, Quaco is believed to have provided intelligence to the Americans who aided in the capture of British general Richard Prescott.

Revolution, many military officials believed women and Black people were less intelligent than white men. Many spies used these stereotypes to their advantage, easily accessing certain secure areas without drawing suspicion.

LYDIA DARRAGH

In 1777, British forces controlled the colonial city of Philadelphia. British general William Howe's headquarters was across the street from the home of local Quaker Lydia Darragh. Quakers had remained neutral in the war. So, the British didn't believe Darragh was a threat and sometimes used her home to hold secret meetings. In December, Howe and his officers met in one of Darragh's rooms. They discussed plans for a surprise attack on American general George Washington's army, stationed at nearby Whitemarsh. Darragh, who was listening through a keyhole, heard every word. She rushed to pass the intelligence to an officer stationed at Whitemarsh. When Howe's forces came, Washington was ready.

Darragh delivered a coded message with information of the attack to Washington's forces while pretending to get flour from a nearby mill.

Lincoln (*left*) relied on telegraph technology so much, he was known to sleep in the telegraph operator's office during important battles.

CHAPTER 4

LIGHTNING MESSAGES AND SPY BALLOONS

US PRESIDENT ABRAHAM LINCOLN SPENT MUCH OF THE Civil War hunkered down in the telegraph office in Washington, DC. From there, he could communicate with his generals on the front lines, strategizing and directing troop movements. He also sent telegraph messages to journalists and newspapers, hoping to control the narrative around the war. But the telegraph also served another purpose for Lincoln beyond communication—surveillance.

In 1862, Lincoln passed a law allowing his secretary of war, Edwin Stanton, to intercept any telegraph messages. Messages were routed through Stanton's office, where they were analyzed and then forwarded to their intended recipient. A team of codebreakers was on hand to decipher any encrypted messages. And if a telegram was particularly damaging to Lincoln or the war effort, it sometimes didn't reach its intended destination.

LISTENING IN AND TAPPING WIRES

Lincoln didn't just use the telegraph to spy on political leaders and the Confederate military. He also used it to spy on Americans. By reading the private messages of civilians, Union leaders could understand what people thought and felt about the war. Lincoln could even control what was published by arresting journalists who

THE TERRIFIC TELEGRAPH

The telegraph was invented by American painter Samuel F.B. Morse in 1837. Morse developed a code based on a system of dots and dashes that represented letters and numbers. A transmitter sent the dots and dashes, in the form of short and long electric pulses, through a wire from one telegraph station to another station. There, the message was decoded by a telegraph operator. By 1861, telegraph wires stretched across the US, making instant long-distance communication possible.

The first message ever sent by telegraph was on May 24, 1844. It said, "What hath God wrought."

revealed themselves to be pro-Confederacy through their telegraph messages.

The Union had far more telegraph lines than the Confederacy. But the Confederates used the technology to their advantage. In 1862, Union telegraph operator David Homer Bates noticed an unusual pattern of telegraph signals coming from Union general Ambrose Burnside's headquarters. Like handwriting, each telegraph operator had a unique style. But the pattern of this signal didn't match that of any Union telegraph operator Bates knew.

Bates was one of the first operators in the US Military Telegraph Corps, which maintained communications between the Union government and its army.

Bates realized a Confederate spy had tapped the line. This meant the spy attached an instrument to the line that could detect electrical pulses. They could not only intercept telegraph messages, but also send messages. Bates sent Burnside's telegraph office a series of fake messages for the spy to intercept. Burnside also sent troops to search along the line for the spy, but they were long gone when the troops arrived.

AERIAL OBSERVATION

The telegraph wasn't the only surveillance technique used during the Civil War. In 1861, civilian balloonist Thaddeus Lowe realized hot-air balloons could provide the Union with a new way to gather intelligence. From the sky, a balloonist, known as an aeronaut, could get an aerial view of troop movements, numbers, weaponry, and more. Lowe convinced Lincoln to add hot-air balloons to his intelligence operations. In July, the Union Army Balloon Corps was officially formed, with Lowe as chief aeronaut.

The Union Army Balloon Corps had seven balloons that could ascend to 1,000 feet (300 m) in the air. From there, aeronauts could view activity as far as 7 miles (11 km) away. They used signal flags or telegraphs to send the intelligence they gathered to generals on the ground. The balloons were usually tethered to the ground, but occasionally an aeronaut would take a balloon on a free-flight mission. This was dangerous because the balloon might drift over Confederate lines.

The Confederate army also used spy balloons. But Lowe's highly organized Union Army Balloon Corps was better funded and more successful than its Southern counterpart. To evade spy balloons and hide their

The largest Union balloon could carry up to five aeronauts. Lowe's favorite balloon was the *Intrepid*, which was used to view the Battle of Fair Oaks.

THE FIRST SPY BALLOON

The Civil War was the first conflict to make widespread use of spy balloons. But balloons had been around long before then. French brothers Jacques-Étienne and Joseph-Michel Montgolfier created the first hot-air balloon in 1783. France first used balloons for surveillance during the French Revolution. French aeronauts flew a hydrogen balloon for ten hours to observe Austrian troop movements during the 1794 Battle of Fleurus. France won the battle, but its balloon corps was disbanded soon after.

The Montgolfier brothers first demonstrated their balloon on June 4, 1783, in Annonay, France. It rose about 3,000 feet (914 m) into the air for about 10 minutes.

numbers, Confederate leaders blacked out their military camps at night. This meant their troops weren't allowed to use any visible light. The Confederates also created fake camps and military equipment to trick the aeronauts. These tactics sometimes worked, but they took a lot of time and resources.

The Confederates surrendered in 1865, ending the Civil War. But the use of surveillance balloons was just beginning. And new technology would change the world of surveillance forever.

When the HMS *Diana* intercepted Russian Navy high-frequency radio communications, the crew learned that Tsar Nicholas II was moving his ships to the Pacific Ocean.

CHAPTER 5

WARTIME TECH

ON JANUARY 28, 1904, THE CREW OF GREAT BRITAIN'S HMS *Diana*, stationed in the Suez Canal in Egypt, made a startling discovery. The ship's operators could listen in on radio conversations among Russian naval officials using their new wireless Marconi radios. By doing this, the HMS *Diana*'s crew learned that Russia was mobilizing its naval fleet. They quickly passed the information to British intelligence officials, who shared it with Japan, an ally they knew would be interested in this intelligence.

Since the mid-1800s, Russia had been trying to expand its territory east. During the same period, Japan was pushing to expand to the west. This put the two countries in direct competition for the same territory. The movement of Russian ships signaled war. In February, Japan launched a surprise attack on Russian naval forces, starting the Russo-Japanese War.

The HMS *Diana*'s interception of Russian radio signals was the first use of SIGINT in wartime. But

Marconi received the Nobel Prize in Physics in 1909 for his work in developing wireless telegraphy.

it wasn't the last. Throughout the war, Japan relied on intercepted radio communication to learn where its enemy was and what the enemy was doing. A little over a year later, Russia surrendered.

RISE OF RADIO

At the time of the Russo-Japanese War, wireless technology was still relatively new. In 1894, Italian inventor Guglielmo Marconi developed a wireless communication system that could send messages using radio waves, a type of electromagnetic radiation. These waves of energy carried electronic signals through the air. Marconi built devices that used these radio waves to send messages wirelessly. Wireless communication offered huge advantages over telegraph communication because it didn't rely on lines and stations. It was highly mobile and could be used on ships and airplanes. These advantages made it a primary method of communication during World War I.

WARTIME WIRELESS

World War I wireless operators could send and receive messages from anywhere in the world. All they needed was a transmitter and a receiver. But the rise of radio technology also created new security threats. Anyone listening on the same frequency could intercept the wireless signal. That meant the enemy could hear any wartime messages. So militaries encrypted their messages to protect their secrets. Cryptographers on each side developed increasingly complex codes and ciphers to protect secret information. Meanwhile, talented codebreakers worked to decrypt their enemy's messages.

World War I ended in 1918. But in 1939, World War II broke out. Advances in technology helped spies on both sides stay one step ahead of their enemy.

During World War II, the Germans used a machine called Enigma to encrypt their messages. British mathematician Alan Turing created a machine called Bombe (*pictured*) to help decode Enigma.

HISTORY OF THE NSA

In 1917, the US officially declared war on Germany, joining the Allies in World War I. A few weeks later, the US government set up its first SIGINT organization, a code and cipher division dedicated to intercepting and decoding enemy communications. In 1952, US president Harry Truman officially formed the NSA. The NSA is responsible for cryptology, global communications monitoring and analysis, and protecting the security of US communications systems.

THE FIRST SPY CAMERAS

Visual surveillance using photography became a popular tactic throughout both World Wars. During World War I, pilots flew planes with cameras mounted on them to do aerial reconnaissance. By World War II, intelligence agencies began using spy cameras.

Robert D. Gray invented the first commercial spy camera in 1885, called the Concealed Vest Camera.

The NSA is the most secretive US intelligence agency. The US government didn't even admit it existed until 1975.

The camera was designed to be hidden in a vest pocket with the lens concealed in a buttonhole. Gray's camera could produce six small, round photographs. It was a popular novelty but wasn't widely used by professional spies. It was the Minox spy camera that got a starring role in espionage during World War II.

THE MARVELOUS MINOX

In 1936, German inventor Walter Zapp created the smallest 35mm camera on the market. The subminiature camera, which later became known as the Minox, was only 3 inches (8 cm) long. It could fit into the palm of a spy's hand or be slipped into a coat pocket. The Minox was able to focus on nearby objects, a challenge for many small cameras at the time. While the camera was intended to be a luxury item for civilians, it quickly caught the attention of intelligence agencies around the world. By the time World War II ended in 1945, spies on both sides were using the

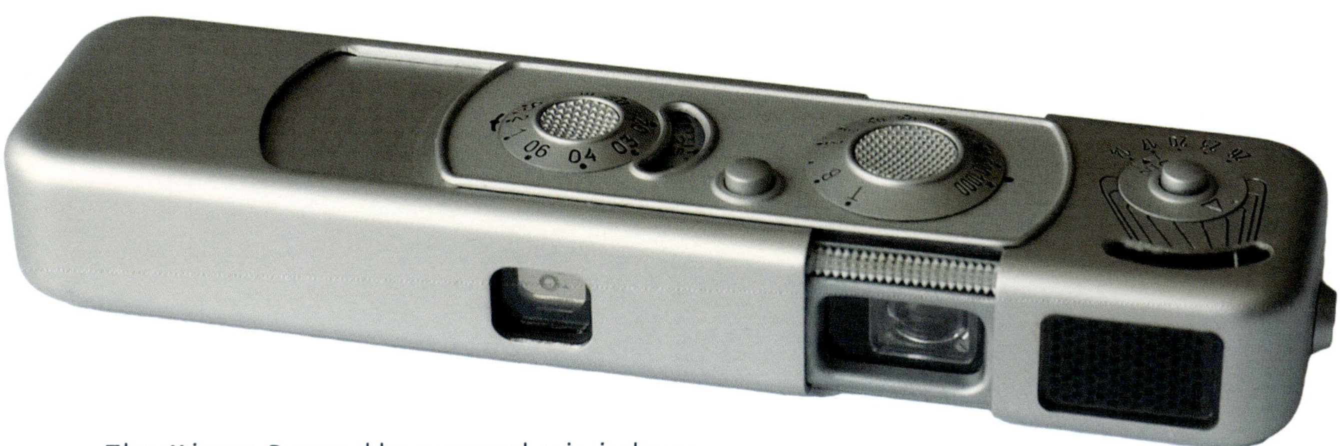

The Minox B was the second miniature camera produced by Minox. During its 14-year production, it was the company's most popular camera.

PIGEON SPY CAMERAS

Homing pigeons were also used for surveillance during both World Wars. But these birds became especially useful during the Cold War. Each pigeon wore a tiny harness with a battery-operated camera programmed to automatically take pictures at timed intervals. The equipment weighed just over 1 ounce (28 g), so it wouldn't impact the bird's flying ability. Spies released the pigeons over targets, where photos could be taken of troop numbers, movements, weapons, and more. Pigeons are always able to find their way home. So they could be released anywhere, returning to their handlers carrying valuable intelligence.

In the 1970s, the CIA used pigeon cameras to take photos during the Cold War. They code-named the operation Tacana.

Minox to capture photos of secret documents, weapons, and other intelligence.

World War II ended with a divided Germany. East Germany was allied with the USSR. West Germany was allied with Europe and the US. This caused great distrust between the two sides, setting the stage for the Cold War. During the Cold War, the US and its allies competed against the USSR and its allies for technological and military superiority. These countries never openly fought one another. Instead, the nations waged secret battles using information to keep their rivals from gaining too much power. Spies were their

Because of its size and shape, the Minox could be hidden in a small object, such as a shoe brush.

US INTELLIGENCE ORGANIZATIONS

The FBI was founded in 1908 to combat crime. It enforces US laws and gathers intelligence from US citizens. The CIA was founded in 1947 to gather foreign intelligence. The CIA is not allowed to gather intelligence from US citizens and is not allowed to act on any information it receives. Instead, CIA officials must share the intelligence with law enforcement agencies or government leaders.

intelligence agencies' eyes and ears on the ground. And cameras were key to their intelligence operations.

CAMERA CONCEALMENT

Throughout the Cold War, those on both sides of the conflict worked to understand the plans and intentions of their enemy. During this time, the intelligence industry thrived with hundreds of thousands of spies working to gather enemy secrets. Countries around the world established and grew their intelligence agencies to manage their espionage activity. For the USSR, it was the KGB and GRU. Britain had MI6. And the US had the FBI and the CIA.

For spies, secrecy and efficiency are key to surveillance. Soviet and US intelligence agencies worked to develop the latest and greatest spy cameras. Finding creative ways to conceal cameras became an art. Cameras were concealed in umbrellas, cigarette boxes, matchboxes, and more. To make a matchbox camera more

The Eastman Kodak Company created matchbox cameras during World War II. They were used by resistance personnel.

convincing, the spy could even replace the cover with a local hotel or restaurant matchbox cover.

The TROPEL camera was another subminiature camera like the Minox. The handmade camera was concealed inside a pen and was famous for its ability to capture documents. It contained a series of glass lenses, allowing it to capture documents with almost perfect clarity.

The Tessina camera was created by the CIA. It was a spring-wound 35mm camera that could fit in a cigarette pack or be used as a body camera.

« SPY HALL OF FAME »

ADOLF TOLKACHEV

Adolf Tolkachev was a Soviet military engineer who became one of the CIA's most successful Cold War spies. When his wife was a child, Soviet leaders executed her family. Motivated by revenge, Tolkachev began spying for the US in 1980. He worked as an airborne radar specialist for the Soviet military. As a result, he had access to classified documents containing Soviet weapons technology information.

Using his TROPEL camera, Tolkachev photographed detailed plans and maps for future weapons and gave the photos to the US. The US military used the plans for their own weapons, saving billions of dollars in research and development. In 1985, Soviet intelligence agencies discovered Tolkachev's espionage. He was arrested and executed soon after.

The TROPEL camera was hidden in the back of a fountain pen. The end could be unscrewed, revealing the camera lens and allowing the spy to take photos.

SOVIET INTELLIGENCE ORGANIZATIONS

During the Cold War, the USSR had two main intelligence organizations, the GRU and the KGB. The KGB was the intelligence organization for the USSR's Communist Party. It gathered foreign intelligence, often through espionage. But the organization also acted as a secret police force during the Cold War. The KGB ended with the collapse of the USSR in 1991. The GRU is the highly secretive foreign intelligence organization for the Russian military. Like the KGB, it uses spies, but less is known about its operations. And unlike the KGB, the GRU is still in operation.

Created in 1954, the KGB was meant to serve as the "sword and shield of the Communist Party."

Cold War spies also found ways to hide cameras on their bodies. Body cameras could be concealed inside a purse, belt, or bra strap. Spies could activate a camera by putting their hands in their pockets or touching a purse strap. Spies used these cameras to capture images of meetings, allowing intelligence agencies to see who was meeting whom. But the cameras didn't have the ability to record audio. For that, intelligence agencies turned to the most famous piece of Cold War spy tech, the small but mighty bug.

The Vladimir Lenin All-Union Pioneer Organization, a similar organization to the Boy Scouts, gifted the wooden carving of the US seal to Harriman.

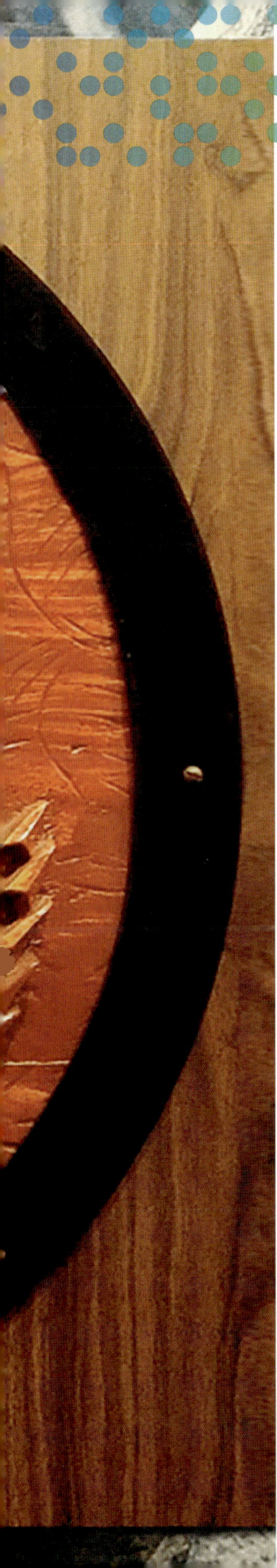

CHAPTER 6

BUGS AND SUBS

IN 1945, US DIPLOMAT W. AVERELL HARRIMAN, WHO WORKED at the US embassy in Moscow, received a gift. A group of boys from a Soviet youth organization presented the ambassador with a handmade wooden carving featuring the US seal. The gift symbolized friendship between the USSR and the US.

Given the mistrust between the two countries, US intelligence agencies would have typically checked the gift for recording devices. But the carving appeared to be solid wood containing no electronics, batteries, or wires. Harriman was delighted. He hung the carving in his office, where it stayed for the next seven years.

In 1951, US radio operators came upon Harriman's voice being broadcast over the airwaves. US intelligence officials scanned Harriman's office for bugs but found nothing. Eventually, they traced the bug to the carving and nicknamed the listening device "the Thing." But they still had no idea how it worked.

THE THING'S MYSTERY

Inside the carving, US intelligence agency engineers found a hollow space containing a small metal antenna with a cylinder on top. They quickly got to work analyzing the Thing. The device had no power source, yet it could still broadcast.

In 1952, British scientist Peter Wright uncovered the Thing's secret. The Soviets were sending an electromagnetic signal at the Thing from a listening post outside the embassy. A thin membrane on the cylinder inside the Thing picked up the vibrations created by human speech and carried them to the antenna. When the Soviets' signal struck the antenna, it briefly gave the Thing enough power to transmit the vibrations to the listening post.

The Thing was created by Russian inventor Leon Theremin, who made the device while at a secret lab in a Soviet prison.

The Thing was an example of a passive cavity resonator. This type of bug, or secret listening device, could operate without a power source. It was new to US intelligence officials at the time, but it wasn't the first bug. Intelligence agencies had been bugging one another since the Cold War began.

KITTY SURVEILLANCE

Pigeons weren't the only animals recruited as spies during the Cold War era. Intelligence officials knew that animals could often go places a human spy couldn't. And no one would suspect a cat sunning itself on a windowsill to be a CIA spy in disguise. During the Cold War, the OTS experimented with turning cats into bugging devices. A veterinarian placed a microphone in the cat's ear that connected to a transmitter located at the base of the animal's skull. The electronics were powered by a battery pack inside the cat's ribcage. However, the batteries were too small to last long and training the cats was too difficult. Eventually the OTS abandoned the project, nicknamed Acoustic Kitty.

The OTS only experimented with one cat. After its testing proved Acoustic Kitty was not practical, the project was discarded.

A BUGGY BUILDING

Bugs are fairly simple devices. They usually only consist of a radio transmitter with a microphone. But this simplicity means a bug can be unbelievably small and hidden in anything. During the Cold War, intelligence agencies were known to hide bugs in shoes, bullets, clocks, and more.

In 1979, construction started on a new US embassy building in Moscow. But after the typewriter bugs were found in the other embassy building, the US was concerned. In 1985, the new embassy was 65 percent complete when construction abruptly stopped because US security officials realized the entire building was bugged. The building remained unfinished and empty for years.

In 1992, after the Cold War ended, the Russian government allowed the US to finish the embassy. However, US security experts knew it would never be truly secure. US construction workers tore down the

Multiple gap-jumping antennae were found in concrete columns in the US embassy. The antennae connected to each other magnetically, allowing the Soviets to transfer data without a wired connection.

BUG DETECTION

For many Cold War intelligence officials, finding their enemies' bugs was a full-time job. Teams of specially trained engineers routinely searched classified locations for clues that their security was compromised. For example, if a section of wiring had a suspicious voltage, it might mean a microphone was attached to it. A receiver could scan rooms, searching for any transmitting bug. Telephone analyzing devices could also help determine if a foreign agency was listening in to phone calls.

top three floors of the embassy and added four new stories using materials imported from the US. Once construction was finished, low-level work was done on the building's unsecured lower floors. All classified work was done on the US-built floors.

OPERATION IVY BELLS

During the Cold War, bugs weren't the only new technology to become popular. Submarines had been around since the 1700s, but they didn't gain widespread use until the rise of diesel, and later nuclear power, in the 1900s. By the 1950s, spy submarines were on the front lines of the tension between the US and the USSR.

In 1972, the US Navy undertook an especially daring underwater espionage mission. US intelligence officials had discovered an underwater cable connected to a Soviet naval base on the Siberian

coast near the Sea of Okhotsk. It ran to another naval base near the USSR's border with China and North Korea. Soviet military personnel used it to communicate with officials in Moscow. Because of the cable's remote location, the Soviets didn't encrypt their communication. If the US could tap the cable, it could listen in on everything the Soviets were saying.

The top secret mission, code-named Operation Ivy Bells, used a nuclear-powered submarine called the USS *Halibut,* which sat on the ocean floor, 400 feet (120 m) below the surface. Navy divers left the submarine and walked along the seafloor until they reached the

Only a few people on the USS *Halibut* knew about Operation Ivy Bells. The rest of the crew thought they were recovering debris from a sunken Soviet anti-ship cruise missile.

cable. They installed a clamp on the cable containing recorders that captured any communication going through the cable. If the Soviets ever needed to bring the cable to the surface for repair, the clamp would automatically detach.

Operation Ivy Bells was a success, providing the US with years of useful intelligence. In 1980, an NSA spy revealed the operation to the Soviets, who found and removed the clamp, ending the project. Still, many experts say the intelligence gained during Operation Ivy Bells helped end the Cold War.

China sent the balloon over the Malmstrom Air Force Base in Montana, which is where some of the US nuclear assets are stored.

CHAPTER 7

EYES IN THE SKY

ON FEBRUARY 1, 2023, CHASE DOAK OF BILLINGS, MONTANA, noticed a strange object in the sky. It appeared to be a huge white circle hovering above Billings. Thinking it could be a UFO, Doak took pictures of the object and posted them to social media. The post quickly went viral. Officials at the US Department of Defense (DOD) were tracking the object as well. They sent jets, including a U-2 spy plane, to get a closer look.

The object was a balloon, about the size of three school buses, floating about 60,000 feet (18,000 m) above Earth. It had traveled over Alaska and Canada before entering US mainland airspace. DOD officials determined the object was a Chinese spy balloon, sent to capture aerial surveillance of US military sites.

THE SPY BALLOON

Chinese officials claimed the object was a weather-monitoring balloon that was blown off course. But as DOD officials examined the

A team of US Navy sailors retrieved the balloon from the ocean after an F-22 fighter jet shot it down.

balloon from the air, the evidence was hard to ignore. The balloon carried a lot of surveillance equipment. Most weather balloons are propelled by the wind and can't be steered. However, this balloon contained a series of motors and propellers that allowed controllers to maneuver it over specific sites.

The DOD tracked and studied the balloon as it traveled across the US. When the balloon reached the coast of South Carolina on February 4, a US fighter jet shot it down over shallow ocean water. US Navy divers quickly recovered the debris for further study.

The drama surrounding the spy balloon captivated people around the world. It also alarmed US intelligence officials, who were concerned with how long it took for the DOD to spot the balloon. In an age of spy planes, satellites, and drones, many people were

The U-2 Dragon Lady aircraft has been in service since 1956.

surprised to learn an espionage technique from the Civil War era could be so effective. In the weeks after the balloon incident, the US Air Force shot down four additional suspicious balloons in US and Canadian airspace. It seemed spy balloons were everywhere.

SPYING FROM SPACE

Spy balloons have some advantages over high-tech aerial surveillance devices. They are inexpensive and can capture images and electromagnetic information close to the ground. And with

U-2 SPY PLANE

Since the Cold War, most aerial reconnaissance was done by satellites or drones. But spy planes have an important place in US history. The most famous spy plane, the U-2, was developed in the 1950s for high-altitude surveillance, above 70,000 feet (21,000 m). At this elevation, the pilot had to wear a special pressure suit and oxygen mask. The plane included cameras, signal-intercepting equipment, and mapping equipment. At the time it was built, the U-2 was the most advanced form of aerial surveillance available.

In the 1960s, the US launched its first spy satellite. It detected radar from the USSR, sending the information it received to the US to be decoded and evaluated.

so many weather balloons drifting through the sky, they can be difficult to spot. But for most intelligence agencies, their favorite tool for aerial espionage is the satellite.

Most spy satellites orbit between 600 and 1,200 miles (1,000 and 1,900 km) above Earth's surface. Even from this incredible distance, satellites can capture almost any type of intelligence. They have high-resolution cameras that take detailed photos and radar used to study military sites. Equipment on satellites can also intercept radio signals and detect weapon deployments, such as missile launches.

DRONE POWER

Although spy satellites are an important tool for aerial espionage, they are expensive to build and can take years to launch. Once in orbit, it can be hard or even impossible to maneuver a satellite. Drones, on the other hand, can be launched at a moment's notice. They can hover in place over a target and be controlled by an operator on the ground. And some can fly longer than 40 hours at a time. A single drone can also track thousands of targets at one time. They can be as large as a plane or as small as a candy bar.

The Gorgon Stare is one of the most powerful spy drones known to be used by the US military. Its camera can capture motion imagery of a large area, such as a city, and zoom in on a target while recording other images at the same time. The Gorgon Stare's

An unarmed MQ-9 Reaper drone was used to build and test the Gorgon Stare.

IT'S A BIRD, IT'S A ... DRONE

In the mid-2010s, Chinese intelligence officials began using drones disguised as birds. The bird drones, code-named Dove, had flapping wings, GPS, a high-definition camera, satellite-communication equipment, and a flight control system. From the ground, a Dove drone looks just like any other bird. It is so realistic that other birds were spotted flying alongside it. China isn't the only country whose intelligence agencies are experimenting with bird drones. In 2023, US researchers experimented with converting dead birds into drones to study flight patterns and formations. And one day, they may be used for surveillance.

Song Bifeng, a professor at Northwestern Polytechnical University in Xi'an, China, runs the Dove project, which models its drones after doves.

camera has a resolution of 1.8 billion pixels, making it more than 100 times more powerful than a standard smartphone camera.

TODAY'S TECH

From spy satellites to drones, the advancements in surveillance technology show no signs of slowing down. New bugs are almost impossible to find. Laser microphones can detect sound vibrations from a conversation by simply pointing a laser at a window. New technology even allows light bulbs to serve as microphones. The light bulb's pulse frequency varies depending on the sound vibrations from human speech.

Many modern spies also work for corporations.

A telephoto lens then measures these pulses and converts them back into human speech.

The rise of smartphones also opened up a whole new world of digital espionage. Today, about 85 percent of the world's population carries smartphones. These phones contain a lot of personal information, from photos to passwords to credit card numbers. Mini cell towers hidden in airports and other busy locations can download information from a mobile phone before connecting it to a main tower.

New espionage technologies are being developed all the time. Since most espionage activities and technologies are top secret, most of them won't be known until intelligence agencies move on to newer ones. No matter what new surveillance techniques intelligence agencies employ, it's almost certain that their agents have eyes and ears everywhere, working to make the world a safer place.

SO YOU WANT TO BE A SPY?

Spies can be anywhere and everywhere. Your soccer coach, a friend's parent, or even a family member can be a spy! But being a spy who can collect secret intelligence without detection isn't easy. Do you have what it takes to do secret surveillance? Complete the missions below to find out!

MISSION 1 LOOK

WHAT YOU NEED

pencil

paper

Part of surveillance is the ability to know what's happening in an image. Photos may be black and white or out of focus. It's your job to find out what the photo is showing. Study the photo below. Look for details, such as the people, their clothes, and their surroundings. Write a short intelligence report on what you think is happening. Use evidence from the photo to back up any claims you make.

MISSION 2
LISTEN

WHAT YOU NEED

smartphone

assistant

Turn a smartphone into an audio surveillance device. Choose three places in your home, such as under a couch, on a shelf, or under a book. Open the phone's audio recorder application, turn it on, and hide it in the first spot. Then have a conversation with someone in the same room. Don't tell them where the phone is! Repeat for the other two hiding spots. When you're done, review the recordings with the other person. Make sure to delete them afterward! Which was clearest? Did the other person spot your phone?

MISSION 3
DECRYPT IT

WHAT YOU NEED

pencil

paper

The World War II message below was sent using a complex code. It's been simplified to a shifted alphabet code. Each letter is replaced by a letter a fixed number of letters after it in the alphabet. If the code used a shift of four, the letter *A* would be *E*, *B* would be *F*, and so on. The message below uses a shift of seven. Can you solve it?

klahpu CVSVR[cpp] dov pz dvyrpun pu wshua vu LUVYTVBZ, Ol pz h MLSSVDJVBUAYFTHU [GLTSFhR][cppp].

—1944 intercepted cable from New York to Moscow

Answer: detain VOLOK[vii] who is working in plant on ENORMOUS, He is a FELLOWCOUNTRYMAN [ZEMLYaK][viii].

TIMELINE

French king Louis XIV forms a system to intercept and read private letters.
LATE 1600s

1775–1783
The American Revolution

1777
Lydia Darragh spies on British officers and learns of an upcoming attack on George Washington's forces nearby.

French aeronauts use a hydrogen balloon to observe Austrian troop movements during the Battle of Fleurus.
1794

1861
The Union officially forms the Union Army Balloon Corps.

The American Civil War
1861–1865

Abraham Lincoln passes a law allowing Secretary of War Edwin Stanton to intercept and read telegraph messages.
1862

1904
The crew of the HMS *Diana* eavesdrops on Russian radio messages, leading to the start of the Russo-Japanese War.

1914–1918
World War I

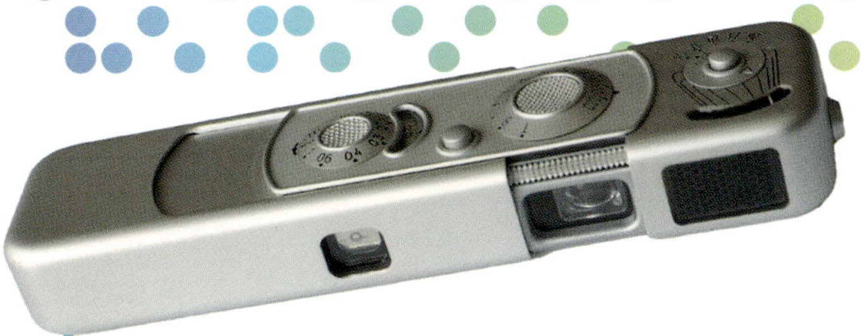

German inventor Walter Zapp invents the Minox spy camera.
1936

World War II
1939–1945

1945
US diplomat W. Averell Harriman receives a carving of the US seal as a gift from the Soviets, not realizing it contains a listening device nicknamed "the Thing."

1947–1991
The Cold War

US Navy divers tap an undersea communication cable in Operation Ivy Bells.
1972

1980
Soviet military engineer Adolf Tolkachev begins spying for the CIA.

1984
Project GUNMAN, led by Charles Gandy, reveals that Soviet intelligence agencies have bugged typewriters inside the US embassy.

1985
The US stops construction of a new embassy building in Moscow after realizing the entire structure has been bugged.

The US tracks and shoots down a Chinese spy balloon that has traveled across the country's airspace.
2023

GLOSSARY

airborne–supported or transported by air.

analyst–a person who determines the meaning of something by breaking down its parts.

Civil War–the war between the United States of America and the Confederate States of America from 1861 to 1865.

clandestine–done in secret.

classified–kept from the public in order to protect national security.

cryptology–the study of codes, or the art of writing and solving them.

decrypt–to change from a set of letters, numbers, or symbols that cannot be understood into words that can be understood.

disband–to break up something that is organized.

eavesdrop–to secretly listen to a private conversation.

encrypt–to convert information or data into a cipher or code to prevent unauthorized access.

espionage–the secret gathering of information on others.

intercept–to interrupt something on its way from one place to another.

maneuver–to move in different ways or directions.

monitor–to watch, keep track of, or oversee something.

narrative–a presentation of a series of events, especially one that promotes certain values or perspectives.

potential–having the ability to occur or be achieved in the future.

reconnaissance–military observation of the enemy.

stereotype–a widely held but overly simple idea about a group.

strategize—to lay out careful plans.

subminiature—much smaller and more compact than standard.

surveillance—close observation of someone or something.

X-ray—an invisible and powerful light wave that can pass through solid objects.

ONLINE RESOURCES

Booklinks
NONFICTION NETWORK
FREE! ONLINE NONFICTION RESOURCES

To learn more about spy surveillance, please visit **abdobooklinks.com** or scan this QR code. These links are routinely monitored and updated to provide the most current information available.

INDEX